WORDS DANCE 13
poetry mag

Summer 2013

Words Dance Publishing
WordsDance.com

WORDS DANCE 13
poetry mag

EDITOR-IN-CHIEF
Amanda Oaks

CONTRIBUTING EDITORS
Rebecca Schumejda
John Dorsey
Jessica Dawson
Jason Neese

© Words Dance 2013

All rights remain with the authors, always.

For more information, including submission guidelines, please visit:

WORDSDANCE.com

COVER ART BY
Tamara Phillips

FEATURED ARTIST
photography by:
Alli Woods Frederick

POEMS BY:

- Clementine von Radics • Jeanann Verlee •
- Alizebeth Rasmussen • A. Razor •
- Sheri L. Wright • Leanne Banks •
- Carrie Rudzinski • Olivia Hamilton Jones •
- Donna-Marie Riley • John Dorsey •
- Ellie Di Julio • Genevieve Salazar •
- Lori-Lyn Hurley • Amanda Oaks •
- Gregory Luce • Heather Bell •
- Desireé Dallagiacomo • Jay Sizemore •
- Meggie Royer • Hosho McCreesh •
- Melanie Faith • Rebecca Schumejda •
- Miriam M. • Shinji Moon •

PHOTOGRAPHY BY:

- Dyamond Robinson-Patlyek • Amy Radbill •
- Patricia Christakos • Kat Falcon •

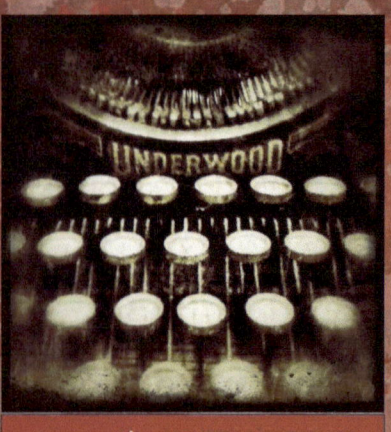

a lost art | ALLI WOODS FREDERICK

cover art by
TAMARA PHILLIPS

Juliana Wigmore Photography

Tamara's art is inspired by the raw beauty of the natural world, resonating cellular life and ethereal wildness. Her detailed watercolour paintings are woven together in earth tones and play with iridescence, challenging the division between subject and environment. Tamara was born on Vancouver Island, British Columbia. She obtained her BSc in Biology from the University of Victoria and currently resides in Vancouver, Canada. An itinerant wanderer, she enjoys both backcountry and world travel, and has called city, sea, and forest her home. Drawing from the subconscious, and filtered through the biological, she investigates our beautiful Earth. :: tamaraphillips.ca

• I believe that being surrounded by beauty and things & people you love is the key to happiness. • I believe in life after death. • I believe that anything, and I do mean absolutely anything, is possible. • I believe that stranger things have happened. • I believe in magic. • I believe a society is defined by the art it creates. • I believe in bigfoot. • I believe pretty is as pretty does. • I believe we exist in the past, present and future simultaneously. • I believe in the UFO coverup. • I believe that love conquers all. • I believe we all have unique gifts and we are responsible for sharing them with the world. • I believe in me. • I believe in you. • I believe in we. • I believe in love. •

featured artist
ALLI WOODS FREDERICK

Alli Woods Frederick is an artist, photographer, author, reiki master, intuitive & zombie survival strategist ™. Her feline companion, Mischa the Wondercat™, is currently being considered for sainthood. She has a deep and abiding love of fancy dress, Bruce Campbell, Bob Hope, big shoes, the 1930's & tea parties... all of which she writes about at KissesAndChaos.com where she invites you to come for the weirdness and stay for the love.

You can view more of her photographic work in her shop or at AlliWoodsFrederick.com.

The Fox has been the subject of many stories in Native American mythology & around the world, much can be learned from both its failures & triumphs. In this case, if we were to judge a book by its cover, we would be recounting an Apache legend that my grandmother passed on to me & you can find retold by Glenn Welker. It tells the story of how the Fox played a key role in introducing fire to the humans. One day the Fox decided to visit the Geese to learn how to imitate their cry. They promised to teach him if he would fly with them, so they thought up a way to attach wings to the Fox, but warned him never to open his eyes while flying. On one of their escapades, darkness fell away suddenly as they flew over the village of the Fireflies. The brilliance below ricocheting off the Fox's closed eyelids caused him to forget & he opened his eyes... his wings crumbled suddenly & he plummeted into the walled village of the Fireflies. In the middle of the village sat a great fire that burned around the clock, this is where the Fox & the Fireflies became quick friends. They told him that if he wanted to leave, he must have the cedar tree bend down & catapult him over the village wall. The Fox decided that he & the Fireflies should have a celebration that night before he left the village. He said, I'll provide the music & you can dance. He tied a piece of cedar bark to his tail & made a drum, possibly the first one ever made, & beat it with his tail while the Fireflies danced. Later, moving closer to the fire & pretending to tire from playing the drum, he handed the drum over to the fireflies to distract them while he lit his tail on fire. He ran to the cedar tree, it bent down to scoop him up & threw him over the wall. He ran & ran, leaving a trail of fire behind him while the fireflies chased him. Finally, exhausted, he gave the fiery bark to a Hawk who carried it to a Crane, who flew far & wide, dropping sparks everywhere.

This is how fire first spread over the Earth.

Fire is synonymous with love, with passion. Fire is truth. Fire is believing in something. Fire is going after what you want. Fire is courage. **Fire is heart.**

Through cunning observation, storytelling, fierceness & a deep passion for wrangling words & arresting images, 24 poets, 5 photographers & 1 painter have unzipped their chests to share their fiery spirits with you, inviting your fire to mingle with their fire.

There's a fire inside all of us & I say, let it burn.

Love,
Amanda

put the kettle on | ALLI WOODS FREDERICK

ADVICE TO THOSE LIKE ME, WITH HEARTS LIKE KINDLING

Darlings, sometimes love will come to you like a fire
to a forest. When it does, be braver than I was. Just leave.
Take only what you can carry. No tears. No second thoughts.
You have hands like tinder boxes, the smallest spark
will kill you.

Get in the car. Pour water on the maps. Avoid gas stations.
Don't look at the flames dancing in the rear view mirror.
Go to new cities, climb on rooftops and slow dance with
your coldest memories. Wallpaper your home with every
dusty, desperate love letter you swore you'd never send.

Find a stranger with sharp edges and uncharted hips.
Press your stories into their skin and forget you ever knew
his name. Just promise me you won't think of burning or
embers. Even when there is ash in your hair. Even when
there is smoke in your mouth.

6 MEMORIES FROM FALLING IN LOVE WITH AN OPTIMIST

i.
Her body made forgiveness
the way mine made blood,
the way it just flowed
when she was hurt.

ii.
We met in the middle
of a riot. She smiled so big
she split my life in half,
into before and after
she turned me into
one of those anarchists
who's really just
hopeful.
Revolutionaries
that in their hearts
are still children with
tree branch swords.
Deep down, she believes
the world is perfectible.

iii.
She told me
there was no such thing
as Destiny.
That I would finally be happy
when I realized there was
nothing in the world
I could not stop or control.

But I think of the night
my drunk hands were useless
at pushing his body away,
and I say you are wrong.
For the sake of my own
survival, you are so,
so wrong.

iv.
The night I held her hands
like worry stones.
I said yesterday
while you were at work,
I looked in your closet for skeletons
and found nothing.
She shrugged,
and said memories
are like family:
you can always walk away.

v.
(On our first date, she said
she hadn't seen her father
since her high school
graduation.)

vi.
The first morning I woke up alone
my mouth held more apologies
than teeth.
I wished my heart was made
of the same stuff as her will,
it would never have broken.

I wished the world was no bigger
than the width of my chest.
There would have been enough
nothing in the world
I would have been enough.
She never would have left.

CLEMENTINE VON RADICS

Clementine von Radics has been published in various magazines and collections, including the first ever poetry feature in Tribu. Her first book, As Often As Miracles, was published by Where Are You Press this past spring. More of her work can be found at clementinevonradics.tumblr.com. She lives in Portland, Oregon.

SWARM

Learn how to say "no."
Cram that word inside your mouth,
the whole thing, make sure all of it
gets in there. Let it walk on your tongue.
Practice with it in the mirror, push it
out, make faces, learn to love the salt
and bitter of it. Teach it to perch on your lip,
buzz, collect pollen from your sugary gloss.
Make it swarm between your cheeks.
Then, when the days come (there will be
many) where he pushes too hard, speaks
too sweetly, when the hand at your thigh
draws a thump in your stomach, when
the bitch gremlin inside whispers 'it's not
worth the fight,' says you can barter
for your worth tomorrow, when your ribs
shrink, when he unfurls his Almighty Smile,
when four come at you at once, when
you love someone else, when the bar
is closing and your name becomes 'Take
What I Can Get,' when the girls hate you
anyway, when you want him until the burn
if only he wore a different face—
pull back your lips, bare the teeth you have
sharpened to their perfect points, flick
your stinger tongue, set free your swarm.

JEANANN VERLEE

from *Racing Hummingbirds* (Write Bloody Publishing, 2010)

THE GREAT HUSH
after the parting

At the dinner party, nine near-strangers crowd around at table two sizes too small, sipping on wine and dipping morsels into sauces, chatting about 1970s films and the proper methods for chopping beets and salting pork. After the first course, someone mentions your name. The room falls to a hush. (Poor fool has no idea what he has done.) The wine in the glasses begins to rise, the flatbread unrolls and butters itself, napkins fall to the floor, a lobster claw reaches up and snaps off the tip of a man's nose. The wine continues rising up over the lip of each glass, a trout's eye winks at its fork, the chickens in the kitchen cluck and stretch their featherless wings, soup springs from a boy's spoon back into his bowl. The wine soaks through the tablecloth, dripping red pearls onto each tightly-packed thigh. When I clear my throat to answer, the clams on one woman's plate pop up, slap shut their shells and scuttle off across the floor, down Madison Avenue, and from what I can tell, straight back out to the sea.

JEANANN VERLEE

Jeanann Verlee is author of *Racing Hummingbirds*, recipient of the Independent Publisher Book Award Silver Medal in Poetry. Her work appears in *The New York Quarterly*, *Rattle*, *failbetter*, and *kill author*, among others. She is a poetry editor for *Union Station Magazine* and director of Urbana Poetry Slam.

jeanannverlee.com

AN OVERDOSE OF YES

Just to be sure and
rule out all things scary,
for three weeks
she wore a tracking device
that sent her every heartbeat
through space – to where?
she did not know
She went through her days
feeling exposed,
under surveillance,
imagining her heart
as an open book
written in a language she
herself was just beginning to learn
On the other end,
a seasoned, empathetic soul
deciphered the signals...
she could read
between the lines,
she had seen it all before
The diagnosis?
A classic overdose of Yes
Yes to risking and opening
Yes to leaping and deepening
Yes to creating and awakening
Yes to being seen

A heart emerging from its
cocoon of complacency
to dance on the

fringes of fearlessness,
experiencing a few
minor growing pains
as it stretches to
contain all the new life

ALIZABETH RASMUSSEN

Alizabeth Rasmussen is a writer, editor, photographer and baseball mom trying to capture and master the art of being perfectly, imperfectly human. She lives in Bellevue, WA with her 13-year-old son and writes for a number of publications, all of which can be discovered from her online hub, Write. Click. writeclick.me

WORDS DANCE 13
poetry mag

summoning | ALLI WOODS FREDERICK

WordsDance.com

AMUSING

working the words
                        this way & that
      watching where they go
across pages that disappear
into the ether of each breath of the muse
as she smiles, spills her drink on me,
then runs down the hall naked,
                      laughing,
                          the way muses sometimes do

A. RAZOR

A. Razor is a writer who loves to write and has been at it for several decades now. Some of his books are available here, as well as books by other writers that he has edited, PunkHostagePress.com

TEACHING MYSELF TO SMOKE

I fretted a stolen cigarette
between fingers sticky with summer,
learning to drag rebellion through a filter,
let it linger in my lungs
filling the need to defy
the absence of light.

I stoked the ember like a locomotive
that was not stopping anywhere,
driven to follow days laid
one in front of the other like tracks
that led far from fourteen.

SHERI L. WRIGHT

Pushcart Prize and Kentucky Poet Laureate nominee, Sheri L. Wright is the author of six books of poetry, including the most recent, *The Feast of Erasure*. : scribblingsandsuch.com

BARE

Soft, tissue-thin skin, warm
narrow rivers run blue, close
to the surface, pulsing life,
a constellation of pale freckles.

My wrist is bare,

save that one small scar
whose beginning I cannot
remember.

LEANNE BANKS

Leanne Banks is a recovering addict, vegan, single mama of a beautiful 10 year old girl who lights up her soul. She writes to get her insides out.

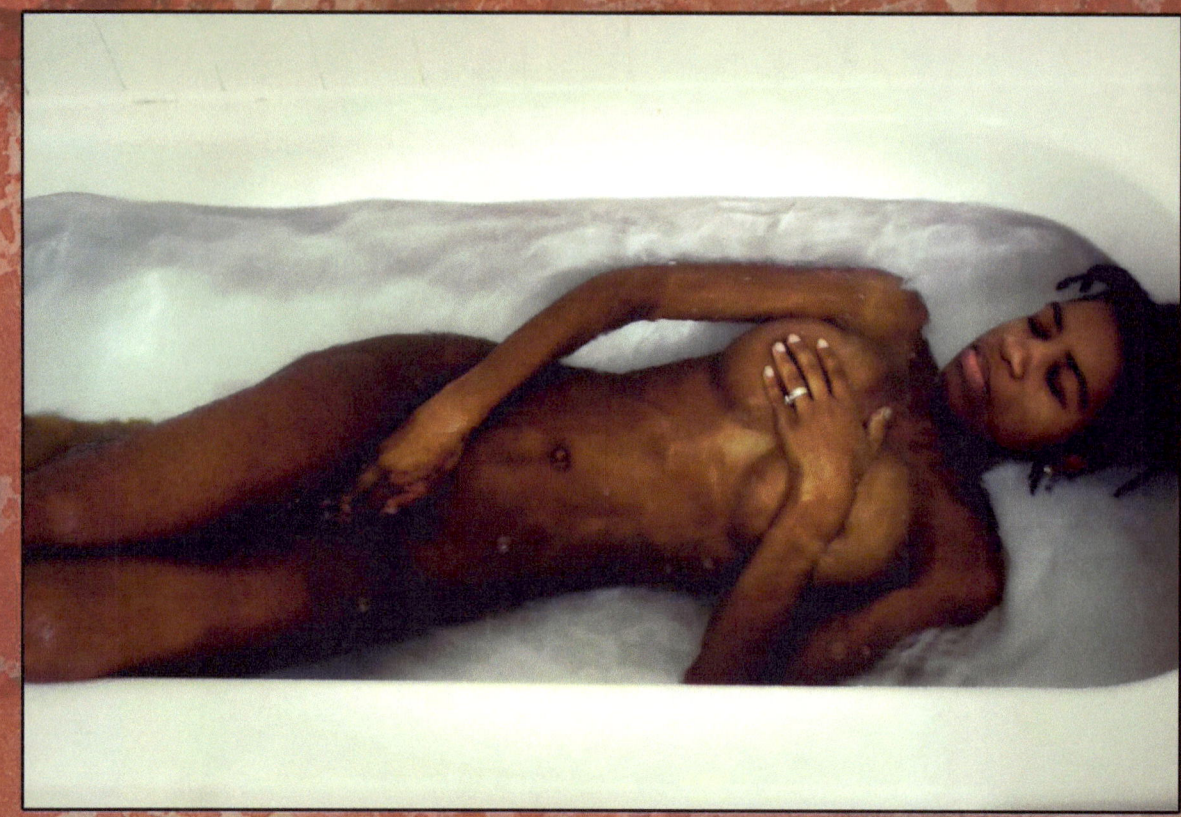

DYAMOND ROBINSON-PATLYEK

Dyamond Robinson-Patlyek is the creative woman behind Shanti Presence - Jewelry for rebellious yogis and spiritual rockstars. This new mama loves cuddling with her puppies, capturing beautiful moments with her camera, and strives to help others see the divine within. Connect with her at her blog: DyamondintheRough.com

IN AMERICA

The first hitchhiker
I ever picked up
I dropped off in the wrong place.
We were both backpackers –
young, dirty, and foreign.
I was so excited to help,
I didn't even realize my mistake
until I was too far
to turn around.
I'd left him on a busy overpass –
gray eyes and tired hands
to search for another way out.

The first time I hitchhiked
I kept my three inch knife
clutched in a fist
inside my bag the whole time.
They were the only ones who stopped:
thick set country boys,
dogs barking in the bed
of their black pick up truck.
I was suddenly so grateful
for my baggy clothes –
my unwashed hair –
their harmless questions –
but I never shook the doubt in my gut –
and I didn't look back when I finally got out.

You could not pay me enough money
to hitchhike in America.

In America, no one looks at you
and everyone stares.

In America, fear is a gender
I am too familiar with.
In America, the street is a river
and all of the men are drowning.

All of the men need you to save them.
All of the men need you.
All of the men have been raised to believe
women are supposed to fuck them.
All of the men expect you to fuck them.
In America, she was asking for it.
In America, I walk with my keys shoved between my knuckles.
All my retorts burn in the wildfire of my throat.
My eyes are sidewalks.
My body: a used noose.
Every voice is a corner —
a dog fight —
a humiliation.

America says, "That poor girl in India —
only in the Third World —
how could six men rape her
and no one do anything?"

In America, I walk down the street
and a boy leans out of his car
to scream "Yo Slut! Pull your hood down!"
In America, I am with my boyfriend
when a man hisses in my ear
"Hey sexy"
so that he and I have a secret.
So that he and I are he and I.

So that I will flinch when the next man
stares for too long.
In America, a man pretended to masturbate on me
during a poetry show
because I was too much talk
and not enough take.
Because my mouth was a siren –
A hive –
Because no one called him
a misogynist after the show but me.

In America, we are taught
to scream the word "FIRE"
if being assaulted because no one
will help us if we yell "RAPE."
No one can see themselves
but we are all looking.

In America, six members
of the high school football team
can show photos of the girl
they pissed on
and raped
and no one will do anything.
Their male authority figures will condone it.
Rape is an American Past Time: A National Sport.
In America, she shouldn't have gotten so sloppy.
In America, boys will be boys.
In America, twenty-two elected Senators can oppose
The Violence Against Women Act.
In America, when you type the word rape
into Google the first option to pop up

is RAPE JOKES.

In America, my body belongs
to the first person who demeaned it:
the boy who broke up with me
because I wouldn't have sex with him.
The one who taught me to find something
to burn. To mold. To shrink. To hate —
My worth stolen like a bicycle in the night —
a yellow blur in the dark.

In America, I am always searching
for another way out.
In America, I am always on fire.
I am always on fire.

THE BED

When he finally confesses
he has been sleeping with her
since he met my parents,

I stop saying his name.
I understand the importance
of existing inside of myself —
the nightmare of being alive.
When he finally evaporates

off my skin,
he leaves behind her scent:
an unscratchable itch.
A gift I gnaw at every night.
Her name is a newborn
the family keeps passing around.
She won't stop growing.
At my birthday, someone exclaims
how she's learning to wear her body
like a crown.

I carve her name into benches.
Bake her eyelashes into my breakfast.
Find her hair in my throat.

Discover she loves everything
I love.

Her mouth is a garden of lies.
I sleep at the foot of her bed.

— CARRIE RUDZINSKI

His bed. The bed
I found her hair in —
wrapped up in the comforter —
a long, blonde, noose —
something I threw aside
when he wasn't looking —
the first lie I told myself.

CARRIE RUDZINSKI

Named "Best Female Poet" at her first national poetry competition, Carrie Rudzinski has since performed her work for audiences across the United States, New Zealand, Australia, and India. She represented the Boston Poetry Slam at the 2010 Individual World Poetry Slam, twice at the National Poetry Slam, ranked 14th at the 2011 Women Of The World Poetry Slam, and placed 2nd at the 2011 NPS Underground Individual Competition. She most recently represented Denver's Mercury Cafe at the 2013 WOWPS. Her newest collection of work, *The Shotgun Speaks*, was published in May 2013.

PROMISE

You will meet her –
She
who carries
your fear, shame, self-doubt –

along the way to
your Truth.

Over and over,
She will drag
her bounty
to your door,
fists full.
"Mend these"
on her lips.

Don't shy away from her.

Open the door wide.
Love her up.
Cook her dinner.
Hear her story.
Ask what she needs.

Wrap Grandmother's
warmest quilt
around her
when she cries.

Place
your hand
on her knee.
Say,
 "I see you."

Then, rise,

take her by the hand
and go and do
precisely what it is
you need to do.

OLIVIA HAMILTON JONES

OLIVIA HAMILTON JONES

Olivia Hamilton Jones - part Writer, part Birth and Pregnancy Coach, part South Philly Mama - is the creator of NoWallsUp.com where she writes about Birth, Bioethics, Zen, Mamahood, Sisterhood, Good Divorce, Better Marriage + more. Her mission and her wish for you: living, learning and loving with No Walls Up.

HOW TO LOVE YOUR DEPRESSED LOVER

Last night I thought I kissed
the loneliness from out your belly button.
I thought I did, but later you sat up,
all bones and restless hands, and told me
there is a knot in your body that I cannot undo.

I never know what to say to these things.
"It's okay." "Come back to bed."
"Please don't go away again."

Sometimes you are gone for days at a time
and it is all I can do not to call the police,
file a missing person's report, even though
you are right there, still sleeping next to me
in bed. But your eyes are like an empty house
in winter: lights left on to scare away intruders.

Except in this case I am the intruder and you
are already locked up so tight that no one
could possibly jimmy their way in.

Last night I thought I gave you a reason
not to be so sad when I held your body like
a high note and we both trembled from the effort.

Some people, though, are sad against all reason,
all sensibility, all love. I know better now.
I know what to say to the things you admit to me
in the dark, all bones and restless hands.

"It's okay." "You can stay in bed."
"Please come back to me again."

FOR JEANANN VERLEE

She writes as if she is full of stone
and a silence that won't sit still any longer.

I wonder how long she has pushed stories
into the cavities of her teeth. After a while,
the secrets we keep start to keep us.

She has a sweet voice until she reads,
a voice of elderflower and honey drizzle.

It is the poems that turn it to scratch.
The poems turn it to salt, turn it to hiss.

Turn to God, they say.
He will love you like a Sunday.
He will love you gentle.
Love you like prayer.

This woman does not need to be loved
like prayer. This woman needs to be loved
like a fist that won't strike, like a mouth
full of spit, like life, like real.

Or else she has had too much of that already.
Or else she has arms like scratch cards,
eyes of flint, a tongue curled up like the ears
of a dog that has been kicked too much
and had it called love.

Or else she doesn't want it at all.
She wants to keep her body like a secret,
wrap it up in silk, in velvet. Who can blame her?

When her body has been used like quicksand.
When her heart has been nailed to bed staffs.
When she has scars she cannot explain.

Who can blame her for her voice like a blizzard,
her voice like a machete that will cut you in two?

Who can blame her for the stones in her body
that make her footfalls heavy where lovers
demand they be light?

A woman like this has no business being light.

Light women are blown off course by gusts
of wind that barely push. A woman like her,
a woman full of stones, she has taken one
blow after another and she is still here.

She is still tall. She wears her spine like
a war medal. She has come home safely,
but she is still prepared to fight.

DONNA-MARIE RILEY

Donna-Marie Riley is a young poet currently residing in Brighton, England. Just recently, she has begun to try her hand at spoken word poetry at various open mic nights around her city. A selection of performances can be found on her YouTube channel and more of her poetry can be seen on her personal writing blog where she has gained a humble following. five--a--day.tumblr.com

she waited for him but he never came | ALLI WOODS FREDERICK

LOCUST STREET GOSPEL

spider used to sit
in the middle of locust street
selling used paperbacks
& sipping on 40 ounces of second hand sunlight
rain or shine
he found religion in the cracks of sidewalks
in the moments spent drinking in   every silver lining
with eternal devotion

he'd just smile
and say, "words are stronger than bones
because you don't have cut your wrists
to know when
they're in your blood."

JOHN DORSEY

John Dorsey is the author of several collections of poetry, including *Teaching the Dead to Sing: The Outlaw's Prayer* (Rose of Sharon Press, 2006), *Sodomy is a City in New Jersey* (American Mettle Books, 2010), *Leaves of Ass* (Unadorned Press, 2011) and *Tombstone Factory* (Epic Rites Press, 2013). His work has been nominated for the Pushcart Prize. He may be reached at archerevans@yahoo.com.

ALIENS AND WRITERS

Being a writer is like being repeatedly abducted by aliens.
You suffer constant episodes of lost time –
"Oh shit, it's 4:15 already? What do you mean, 'it's Tuesday'?!"
You can't get people to believe your stories –
"No, really! A katana-wielding bugbear. Bestseller!"
You feel like you don't belong on this planet –
"How can you possibly hate Catcher in the Rye?!"
And, very occasionally, something's implanted in your ass when you're not looking –
"DAMMIT, CAT, GET OUT OF MY CHAIR!"

ELLIE DI JULIO

Ellie Di Julio is a nomadic writer currently living in Hamilton, Ontario with her Robert Downey, Jr. lookalike husband and their two cats. Between playing Dungeons & Dragons and watching Top Gear, she destroys the kitchen and tries to figure out what it's all about, really. You can find her first novel, *Inkchanger*, on Amazon. elliedi.com *solitary* | **ALLI WOODS FREDERICK**

THIN

When she was young she woke daily
with only the language of grace moistening
her tongue. She believed that she could
survive on choice beams of light, air
sucked through bleached teeth.

Faulty notion, love: thin was never
just a word. Thin is a prayer chanted
from the chapped lips of a head-sick girl
foolish enough to believe that he will want
her if she is hungry for him. Pour the
water, lick the crumbs of saltine

crackers from her fingers. There is
no greater high than blue jeans
hanging off her hips, than blue shadows
lengthening beneath each eye. And
even if the mirror never gives the
fragmentary glimpse of a smile, even
if the phone never rings, isn't it

enough? To have love burrowing
like an ugly cancer into whatever's
left of spring's sweet sixteen flesh,
to be embracing the periphery with
a body so numb it can't feel the drop.

GENEVIEVE SALAZAR

Genevieve Salazar is a writer, poet and artist whose work aims to render visible the shamanic spirit in modern culture and society. Her poetry has been published both in print and online, and she is the author of *The Maniac's Path*, a blog dedicated to the cultivation of healing and support for those suffering from dermatillomania. If she's not writing (which is hardly ever), you can usually find her hunched in a corner with her nose in a thick volume of fairy tales. themaniacspath.wordpress.com

BIRD SIGNS

Once on Palmer Road,
a flock of birds saved my life.
They rose from the left, black smoke,
as one dark wing,
and carved a net in the sky.
I stopped,
dumb-struck,
and saw that the prison that contained me
was of my own construction.
It couldn't be dismantled brick by brick
but had to be demolished
in one great swoop.
There was no way other
than to rise.
I had to take flight,
to push myself forward,
burning what lay behind me,
sacrificing all
but the most raw and fiery chamber
of my heart.
The birds crossed and landed on my right
and a voice rose from my belly,
a voice wholly mine,
which I had never heard,
bypassed my thoughts
and rang like a bell in my throat,

I want out.

LORI-LYN HURLEY

Lori-Lyn Hurley has an MFA in fiction writing from Sarah Lawrence College. She lives as a writer, spiritual intuitive and energy healer in Lexington, Kentucky, with her partner and two pugs. You can find her on her website : lorilynhurley.com

AMY RADBILL

AMY RADBILL

Amy Radbill is a writer, editor, and jewelry designer. She can't seem to shake an obsession with strange, ethereal, fairy-like characters in her self portraits, so she's hoping they at least read more as ethereal-creepy-forest-fairies than glitter-and-unicorn fairies. You can find her at Half-Assed Mama, where she blogs as the child-light half of the Half-Assed Mama team. :
halfassedmama.blogspot.com

MINING ACCIDENTS

1.
The bottom half of my great-grandfather's nose
sat underneath his right eye for most of his life.
Broken, just below the bridge, a mining accident
in his twenties. Sewn up with haste by the hand
of a doctor who didn't think he would survive,
but did. To die at ninety, content & in his sleep,
a year & a half before I was misadventure
in the quarry of my mother's womb.

2.
That one time, when I was trapped for 1,464 days
while my heart caved in all around me. The only way
I made it out of there alive was when I realized that
the only person that could save me was myself.

3.
The day I let the phone dangle off the hook after you
called. Your voice on the other end tripping over
the poppies blooming from your mouth. A cord
stretching across all these years to coil
around my neck. A stash necklace—
still buzzing with a recording in the shallow
of its spoon that I will drill into the hard rock
of my own heart over & over again, a feeling
as familiar as the woman's voice saying:

"We're sorry; you have reached a number
that has been disconnected, please hang up
& try again…"

This is what happens when we don't recognize
the strength in one another. When we lose faith
before we can see the top of their heads as they
crawl up on their hands & knees out of a hole
of hopelessness. When we don't reach out
to kiss them clean.

THE MISGUIDED TEACHINGS OF LOVE

For years I carried them around, tattooed
on the backside of my eyelids.

Every six heartbeats, *blink*. When you
held my wrists, *blink*. The rage that filtered out
from behind your gnashed teeth, *blink*.

The jarring blast of a telephone being slammed
against its cradle again & again, *blink*.

Your father's shotgun resting on your lips
seven-eight-nine- until my eyelashes were
linked together by a lattice of glue that bled
from the cracks of your broken home.

I've walked around for years with your bullshit
ossified in every corner of my glass heart.
Even when I thought that I had scrubbed
every inch of it clean, you show up,
as small as you wanted me to be:

My fingers smoothing over a fresh bruise.
A bubble of jealousy in my throat.
When my eyes glaze over red with anger.
When I see the scar that sits in the middle
of my forehead in the mirror like a tomb
holding the secrets I silently promised
that I would never-ever tell, until the day
I decided to wear my scars
like a crown.

AMANDA OAKS

Amanda Oaks is a digital crusader slogging away to abolish the practice of creatives writing their own bios in the third person. Hi, I'm Amanda Oaks. Creative Minx. Rock-n-Roll Hippie Mama. Poet. Hoop Dancer. Feminist. Multi-Passionate Solopreneur. Creator of Words Dance Poetry Magazine & Enabler at Kind Over Matter. Stalk here : AmandaOaks.com

THE HALF-LIFE OF HUMAN SUFFERING

Residual like the grit
left in a dry stream bed: rough
but it glitters in the moonlight.

GREGORY LUCE

Gregory Luce is the author of two chapbooks, *Signs of Small Grace* (Pudding house Publications) and *Drinking Weather* (Finishing Line Press), and the collection *Memory and Desire* (Sweatshoppe Publications). The father of two sons, he resides in Washington, DC, where he works as Production Specialist for the National Geographic Society. He blogs and would welcome readers there! Connect on Twitter here: @dctexpoet
enchiladasblog.blogspot.com

AFTER LOVE

After you leave for work I open all the windows in
the house. All of them. Even the tiny one over the
shower. After you leave for the supermarket, I dress

up like Kierkegaard. I write similar chain songs
and God-minutes. When you are on the telephone,

I hide behind the sofa and I repeat your conversation
with your mother, lightly and with more gusto: "I am

so sorry I did not become a corporate lawyer or
lobster fisherman! I am so sorry I haven't been

to St. Mary's in sixteen years! Yes, I am terrible,

yes, I hate myself!" While you are changing the

oil, I change the tires around so that you have

to drive sideways down the street. While you

are out at a bar, drowning in Midori Sours like
a chorus girl, I am whispering into the black

box from an airplane that crashed through
our front door: "so many people I love have

given up or gone away, but not you, not you,
not you..." You find me there, sitting with

a bunch of dead people in seat belts, still
and whispering like a scavenger.

— HEATHER BELL

ALL POSSIBLE SIDE EFFECTS

In some cases, it may cause
coma or death. Other cases
include heart disease and rhythm
problems. You may experience

bleeding disorders from the
head or hands. Sudden vision
loss is common, as well as
erections that are painful
and last 4 hours or longer.

When he fucks your best
friend, take one every hour
until you feel chest pain or a
heavy feeling, pain spreading
to the arm or shoulder, nausea,
sweating, and a general
feeling of terror. Ignore the
back aches. Ignore the
curious way he looks in the
store windows as though

the mannequins want
to sleep with him. Ignore
the numbness, everyone has
numbness. When he gives you

flowers, he has also given you
Herpes. Ignore it, you can steal
a new vagina or dick. When you
develop sores in the mouth and
throat, embrace it, a world is

protruding from your chest.
When your headaches worsen,
leave the house like a bird.
Eat leaves and grass. Grab

and bite children. In some
cases, he will take you to the
doctor's, explain your severe
confusion to everyone, and they
will spend the entire time talking
about the skin around your eyes.

Get AIDS to spite him. In
some instances, you will
discover the difference
between fucking and falling

into one another. You're
outside yelling shit fuck
motherfucker. In these
cases, dry mouth is reported.
This is habit forming.
Shit fuck motherfucker.
Shit fuck motherfucker.

In extreme cases, you will
develop seizures and no
one will notice. He hands
you a history of alcohol and
drug abuse. Do not take

before first talking with
a doctor or beautiful woman
or Jesus Christ Himself. You
will soon realize that nothing
exists. Store everything at
room temperature in a closet
safe. Ignore the banging
when he tries to get out.

HEATHER BELL

Heather Bell was nominated for the 2009, 2010 and 2011 Pushcart Prize from Rattle and also won the New Letters 2009 Poetry Prize. Heather has also published four books. Any more details can be found here: hrbell.wordpress.com

the pale | ALLI WOODS FREDERICK

I BREAK LIKE A FEVER

I can't hear anyone talk about love without thinking
plane crash. locked door. snapped matchsticks.

a choir of heartache. Every face, a costume of loss.
Trumpet voices in the second line marching band
out of my funeral home heart.

What I know about grief, I learned in a winter in New Orleans.
Nights I would drive the city, end up by some massive body of water.
Sob at the shoreline. Stare the beast in its face, and it didn't give a shit
how loud I screamed. It roared back louder.
If there is anything that breaking like a wave has taught me,
that grief has curb stomped into my teeth, it is that

When love leaves, it doesn't always
shut the shotgun door on its way out.

The last time I left my heart wide open, the hurricane
in me got so bad the slamming of the stupid screen door
kept me up for months. I couldn't stop pouring out my insides.
I couldn't see the shoreline until I pealed my skin
out of bed, looked straight at it and said *Stupid door.*
You're so fucking loud. Would you quit it already?

I didn't know the carpenters in my heart until I needed 'em.
For 3 months straight, my best friend called me every single morning
just to make sure I was still alive. Because sometimes that is the hardest
thing to do- just stay alive.

On this planet full of zombie hearts.
People walking around pretending to exist.
It looks so god damned easy to play along.

Listen for the people with the upturned palms whispering
Here, take my sweater. It's fucking freezing out there.
You compass. Waterfall smile.
Umbrella chest. Grand canyon elbows.
You deserve to make it home.
Ignore the radio static lost signal hearts
when all you want are directions back
to the lighthouse where your own love lives
through this god damned sea storm.

Keep swimming. The lighthouse. It's there. And it's worth it.
That kind of love only stays when it has to. And it stays every time.

My Mama folded laundry in the hospital that I was born in
so that I wouldn't first see the world as some back road barn in
Oregon.

I come from a heart made from sturdy hands.
A heart made to set sail. Ride the waves.

The storm is always thick. It's always loud. The road home,
it's quiet. It's small. A warm you have to get used to. It's a ship
made from everyone that ever said they loved you and stayed
when your heart slammed shut so loud you could not say it back.

Sometimes, I am so spilling over with feelings
that I have to sit in my room with the lights off
blankets pulled up over my head
so I don't explode out all of my insides.
I am full. I am boiling over. I am fragile.
I am terrified to say that. To say that I am fragile.
I break like a bad habit. Like a fever. a windshield. I break like a wave.

Sometimes love doesn't stay, but motherfuck when it does.
It is worth every fire extinguisher mouth that told you
that you were not enough. It's worth all the people that
tried to put your loves honest flame out.

That confused your birthday candle kiss. Firecracker mouth.
For some blazing forest. torched chapel.

Let 'em run out of you like a house up in flames.
They won't be the first. They won't be the last.
Pull the fire alarm. Let it rain.

ONE SIDE OF AN ON-GOING DIALOGUE WITH SHARON, MY THERAPIST

My father dropped out of high school.
I was the high school.
I might be as crazy as my father, Sharon.

Sometimes when my grief feels
like a mechanical bull, like today,
I want to love anybody but me,
but nobody else wants to ride, Sharon.

The poems, they are anthills inside of my brain.
They won't stop hiding inside of me.
That's why I wear my problems like they are from
the discount bin at a garage sale, Sharon.

People never really leave, they just hide inside of me.
Like my father, my mother on the kitchen floor,
the man's knife in my brother's back in the alleyway
the man's sign outside of the clinic.
That's why my words have to claw from behind my teeth, Sharon.

Why do we keep bringing up my father?
He is a chainsaw in the forest of my bones.
He is a barbed wire fence to my lover's bear hug.
Sharon, why won't he leave? Why won't he come home?

My father. He was a bully. He walked out on our family like we were
detention while the boys put firecrackers in the mouth of my
depression Sharon, being this sad all the time is really hard.

Nobody wants to develop my negatives in their darkroom.

Sometimes, my head is a wishing well
and I fall inside and I'm a coin, flipping like a child.
I don't know how to swim, Sharon.

I swear to God I will break my own heart
clean in half before my lover even cracks it.
I want him to know that, Sharon.
I want him to know that he is made of glue.

Love is a terrifying beast, Sharon.
I hate when people pretend something is what it is not.

When they pretend that watching me implode is love.
It's not love. It's a spectacle. I don't want to be a spectacle anymore,
Sharon.

People are always looking at me.
Who cares that I'm bald? I know I am.
My ex boyfriend's girlfriend is bald.
She was when I met her.
While she was giving him a blowjob in the bathroom of our apartment.

You know, I have a sister that I've never met.
My Mom is not her Mom.
She's the same age as my real sister, Laura.
Her name is Misty.
Do you get it yet? I know, shitty, right?

Sometimes I can feel my heartbeat in my throat.
I swear my heart is trying to tell me mouth
It can't find the right words.
Maybe that's why I yell. I say the wrong things.
I play chicken with myself.
I want to see who is gunna leave.
It's everybody. Mostly everybody leaves, Sharon.

Who doesn't leave?
When I was like, 7, my Mom left.
My brother went to prison when I was 14.
I'm 22, Sharon. He's still in prison. He's still gone.
And now, Sharon, and now he gets mad at me when I don't write him letters.
He left. Why do I have to write him?

Sharon, Why can't I leave?

Sometimes when I get really frustrated I hit the hallway wall.
And I pull my own hair. Maybe that's why I cut it all off.
Yes, I know that anger is always a secondary emotion.
What's the first? Fear. Anxiety. Sadness. Loneliness.

Aren't you supposed to tell me these things, Sharon?
Aren't you supposed to know?

Sharon, it's weird, I cry in doorways all the time.
It's so silly. Why am I standing in a doorway, crying?

That's stupid. I like being alone.
I just hate leaving.

DESIREE DALLAGIACOMO

Desireé Dallagiacomo is a creative writing major at the University of New Orleans where she is a recipient of the Ryan Chigazola Poetry Scholarship. She teaches poetry and performance with Wordplay Teen Writing Project, The Centre for the Arts, and the New Orleans Recovery School District. She enjoys watermelon, estuaries, and disturbing poetry. : poemsbydes.tumblr.com

SEVENTEEN

When I worked at my dad's restaurant,
my hands smelled like onions,
my hair smelled like onions,
my sweat smelled like onions,
such a tart, burning odor,
it kept me awake at night.

The world seemed smeared with a coat of grease,
smudged around the edges, dingy brown,
even after two showers, I felt like a hamburger
squished under a press, my skin a sizzle-pop
mess of burning fat on the grill of adolescence.

One night I served a bully
a handful of my pubes
mixed in with his taco salad,
and I thought about how it felt
to sit on the edge of my dad's bed,
the loaded .38 in my hands,
thinking of reasons to keep living.

JAY SIZEMORE

Jay Sizemore writes poetry because he needs to, his attention span is too short to write novels: blame the internet. He finds a day job to be the enemy of imagination, but poverty is the cruelest of muses. Nashville, TN is where he lives and breathes, in the death throes of modern music.

POEM FOR THE DAY I CUT MY HAIR IN MEMORY OF YOU LEAVING

Because you moved to Canada and left me here with the cat
and a few hundred bags of tea, I now compulsively drink two mugs
every day, with the Irish cream that you liked so much.
My mother's left several messages on your voicemail machine,
wondering how you could break her daughter's heart, but I decided
long ago that I would get your heart tattooed to my palm,
although I'm not sure the tattoo artist has the right color of ink
to match your eyes. Tonight I wake up from the throes of a dream
in which I try to kiss you in a place I've never kissed before,
but every spot is covered.
Here is every pair of boxer shorts you once wore
pressed into amber like insects.
The night is still turning us. I imagine you in Ontario,
alone in a high-rise apartment,
another cat from the local animal shelter curled up in your arms,
your skinny legs covered in its shedding fur.
Two years ago when my hair was at its longest
you told me you'd braid all the stars into it one day if you had
the chance; now it's cropped close to my neck.
Today is spring-cleaning day.
I leave the box on my front doorstep for the mail carrier to handle,
double-wrapped in thick packing tape, your address scrawled
on the upper right-hand label. When you open it,
the strands will sift to the floor like snow.

— MEGGIE ROYER

NOT SO MUCH FALLING IN LOVE AS LEAPING INTO IT

In January my older brother Paul came out without even saying a single word;
I found him wrapped around the body of another boy in the kitchen
when he thought everyone else in the house was asleep,
the two of them slow dancing through the light of the open fridge,
a bag of nectarines rotting sweetly on the marble counter, leaking
dark red sludge like the inner contents of Paul's heart.
In New York City last year a woman was killed while stargazing,
leaning out the window of her apartment to admire the deep pink sky
at the same time a young girl above her leapt from her apartment window,
hitting the woman beneath her, the two of them
plummeting to the earth below, limbs tangled in a lover's embrace.
And that night as I watched Paul tap out a message on the other boy's back
in Morse code at the rate of one letter every five seconds,
dash dot dash dash, dash dash dash, dot dot dash,
I realized that the act of falling in love is not so much a falling
as a desperate, terrifying leap off the highest building around,
the kind of jump that ends in not just a single casualty,
but two.

— MEGGIE ROYER

MEGGIE ROYER

I am 18 years old, from the Midwest, and I have been writing poetry for two of those eighteen years. My main goal is to write poems that pluck at the heartstrings without completely ripping them apart. As for my writing motto, G.K. Chesterton describes my love for words perfectly: "You say grace before meals. But I say grace before I dip the pen in the ink."
:: writingsforwinter.tumblr.com

PATRICIA CHRISTAKOS

Patricia Christakos is an aspiring fine arts photographer. Her first photography exhibition, Finding Wonderland, opens September 2013. To learn more, visit her imaginary hotel : **HalfCenturyMarkHotel.com**. In real life she lives by a lake in Central New York State.

UNTITLED

A coconut margarita
on the 4th of July,
and good christ they're awful,
so sugary
and foo-fooey
and wretched
and cold,
flakes of toasted coconut
spackled to the rim
with drizzled honey, you get
a goddamn brain freeze
just looking at the
hideous thing.

But your buddy
loved them, and after
giving him hours and hours
and hours of merciless hell over it,
him and his girly, umbrella drink,
you being such a big man
what with your brutal Islay Scotches,
and bottles of the old Guinness and all.

"I wouldn't be caught dead
drinking that shit," you said
to him just about every time
he ordered one.

And yet, ever since he died,
you go, twice a year, once on
his birthday, and once on the 4th,
to get one.

And you miss him, of course,
but it's a nice enough way to
remember, suffering through

each god-awful drink,
and you're probably
imagining it, but you're
pretty damn sure that
each time you order one
the waitress scoffs a little,
gives you a crooked eyebrow,
and a smirk like
you gotta be
kidding
me.

UNTITLED

A half-drunk glass
of wine on the headboard
and the hot, warm, sticky
salt of your bodies, the
perfume of a brave and
doubtless lust, sheets tangled,
and she's trembling
beneath you.

The trickle of a
fingertip tracing
a cheek,
a nipple,
a belly button,
sliding down
underneath,
and as you
gently push
into her
you dribble
a swallow of wine
into her warm,
waiting
mouth.

HOSHO MCCREESH

Hosho McCreesh is currently writing and painting in the gypsum and caliche badlands of the American Southwest. He has work appearing widely in print, audio, and online. Find all things Hosho at: HoshoMcCreesh.com

PICA

"Pica is a type of eating disorder in which people have unusual cravings and ingest non-food items such as paper or soap… Pica disorder can vary in severity of items craved, ranging from ice cubes to feces or dirt." - source: treatment4addiction.com.

She likes the earthy taste. Oh,
and the crunch when she chomps
or chips down on the rocks with the ballpeen hammer
stashed behind the ice cream maker box in the garage.
Quartz, slate, limestone, common driveway pebbles.
she's not picky-- just so they have the zinc that gives

a zing. In the a.m. or before work when few are yet up,
she hunches, gathers, spots then stuffs them
into an empty TUMS container, so she can reach
at any time deep into the dark, cool pouch of her purse.
For waiting rooms, picking up her daughter
after school, while shopping for juice boxes and
the family's six o'clock dinner. This, everyday theater.

While most keep mints in rolls of unspooling paper,
she prefers mineral sustenance in bitty chunks
to chew into dusty detritus,
to coat the enamel with this parched covering.
She takes a hit of the tungsten hint, a subterranean kernel
she savors, a flavorsome tang this shame and chomp.

MELANIE FAITH

Melanie Faith holds an MFA from Queens University of Charlotte, NC. Her writing has been nominated twice for the Pushcart Prize. She is a writing tutor at a college prep. high school in Pennsylvania and an online creative writing instructor. Her poems, essays, and fiction have been published in the past year at Vermillion Literary Project, Linden Avenue, Aldrich Press, The New Writer, Foliate Oak, and Origami Poems Project, and her work is forthcoming from Star 82 Review. Her poetry collection, "Catching the Send-off Train," has been chosen as the summer 2013 selection at Wordrunner eChapbooks.

THE REGULARS AT CRAZY EIGHTS

There are men who bet
their paychecks on the flip
of a single card;
mortgage their homes
for a roll of the bones;
chance their car keys
on the nine in the side pocket.

Many of these men go
to church on Sundays and pray
for a big win next time,
for their wives to return,
or for their children to be luckier.
Penniless, these men
throw stones in collection plates.

They come to the pool hall
in lieu of confession
and look to my husband
for absolution.
These men troll the tables
with baited smiles.

Their eyes open like hymnals—
so wide, like the holes
in their stories,
that you can fall
through them
and never hit the ground.

TABLE OF TRUTH

Mikey Meatball's been kicked out
of every pool hall he's ever set foot in.
He's forged checks, harassed patrons,
hustled a small fortune, lost a small fortune.
Once he repeatedly rammed his car
into a guy's truck over a botched bet.

He's been locked up and drugged up.
He blames it all on Agent Orange.
In Vietnam he was an officer;
In Jersey he owned a billiard hall;
In Brooklyn, he owned an Italian delicatessen;
they called him "Papa Meatball."

In Texas, he played a man for his Cadillac
and won, but totaled it on his way back East.
On Haight-Ashbury,
he sold a hookah to a hippie for ten grand
claiming it was Jerry Garcia's.
In Connecticut, he siphoned gas
from some fish's car before
winning his wedding band on the table.

He's a regular in the police blotter,
most recently for whipping his dick out
at a bagel shop owner
for skimping him on cream cheese.
Once he convinced some kid
he shot like shit because
he was using a left-handed pool cue.
Last week, he told me he saw my husband
pick up a prostitute on Broadway,
just to see my jaw drop.
Instead, I responded,

"Well, at least he's getting some."

When Mikey looks into the table,
he sees his own version of reality:
fifteen object balls, six pockets,
and men who will believe anything
he says if there's money on the table.

REBECCA SCHUMEJDA

Rebecca Schumejda is the author of *Cadillac Men* published by New York Quarterly Books in 2012. *Falling Forward* published by sunnyoutside press in 2009 and *Dream Big, Work Harder* in 2006. Her first chap-book *The Tear Duct of the Storm* was published by Green Bean Press in 2001. She earned degrees from SUNY New Paltz and San Francisco State University. She lives, teaches, and writes in New York's Hudson Valley. You can find out more at RebeccaSchumejda.com.

up in smoke | ALLI WOODS FREDERICK

ORDNANCE

the wiry insides
sparking

the ground wet
a mirror

i go up all
artillery shell

bouquet like
iris

unwound and
ready

if i knew how to
spell the sound i make
when i'm excited

i'd put it here

CHASSIS

i remembered him

my right arm
removed at the
shoulder

holding my pen
dumbly
with the left

my torso blown
open with
absence

the way my
rib cage
swung

a cage with
no bird
left

NEW YEAR

it's a wet snow

something swings on
a rusty hinge

there's this giant
invisible white space
surrounding everything

and nothing to do
with my hands

MIRIAM M

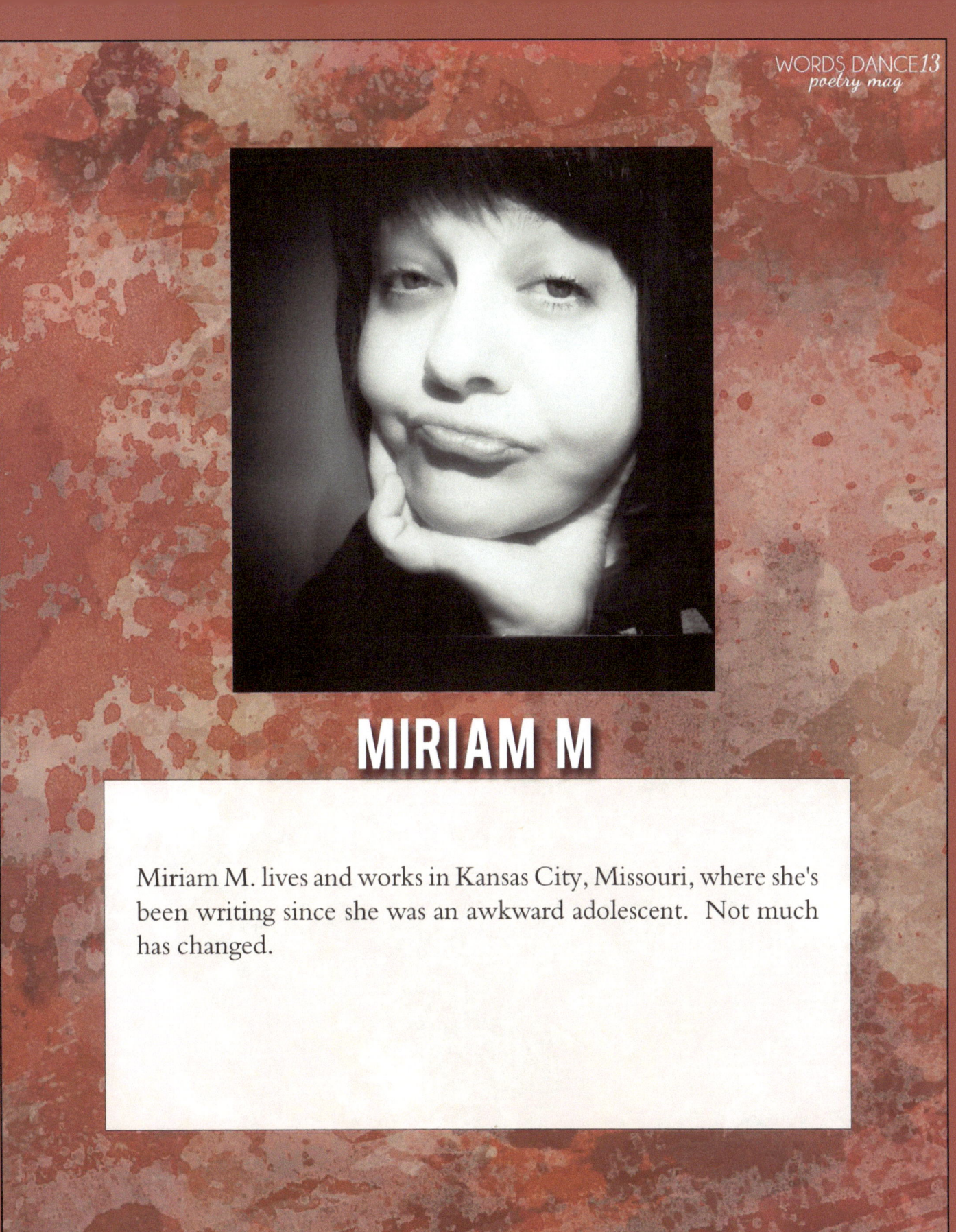

MIRIAM M

Miriam M. lives and works in Kansas City, Missouri, where she's been writing since she was an awkward adolescent. Not much has changed.

KAT FALCON

Kat Falcon is a self-portraiture artist, writer and photographer living in North Texas. She uses her work to tell visual stories, which range from elaborately staged compositions to autobiographical images. Her greatest gift for portrait photography lies with making subjects comfortable being photographed in nontraditional settings.

SELF PORTRAIT

There are certain things about myself
that I romanticize, like the way I have Orion's belt on my chin
or the way my grandmother gave me her hands:
gift-wrapped and covered in flour.

Yesterday, I found a birthmark on my inner thigh
of a heart or spilt milk
and this morning I found that
there's nothing that a person can do
to make me feel more beautiful, than to
trace me like I hold
simpler lines
beneath me.

It's so easy to fool myself into believing that yes,
of course there are constellations on my skin, or
freckles in the night, as if my body
is a pool that reflects the sky.

But all of this
isn't me being a dreamer,
or a spilt-milk, heart-shaped romantic.

It's just me
trying to turn this husk of muscle and dirty fingernails
into something more,

as something
that I can hold like
my grandmother's hands,

as something
I can keep closer to me /
than my own flesh.

THE HISTORY OF WATER

This is the history of water: how it drips through faucets
and touches our skin,

      how the monsoon season floods the Han River
           every summer and swallows one of Seoul's bridges
                      whole.

Every meniscus holds a thousand hands, holds Death and Birth and
whatever may come in between. It remembers how we swam naked
with our bodies made of sixty percent water, the small islands
of our skin surfacing, barely   touching.

We stand naked in the skeleton of my shower, history
pooling sudsy around our ankles — with our skin like oil against the
rain — holding ourselves together as dewdrops collect on the foliage
outside of our windows back home. We kiss, and our mouths collect
sin and miracles, faith and piss — four hundred wars
cleaning the dark hoops beneath our eyes.

We wash each other clean with the dark bones of
secrets, of loss, of famine and fall and friends like us who became
lovers by accident, as

      magnolia suds collect like salt dunes by our toes; Our
feet pressing against the sand, the tide cleaning but never
forgetting,

Water repeating itself again and again, our ghosts clogging up
every drainpipe in this city.

— SHINJI MOON

SHINJI MOON

Shinji Moon is an eighteen year old girl who is no longer afraid of her shadow. She studies English, Journalism, and Creative Writing at NYU and hopes, one day, to write her way out of dying. : commovente.tumblr.com

the masks we wear | ALLI WOODS FREDERICK